M000098772

MATH
Expressions
Common Core

Dr. Karen C. Fuson

GRADE

5

Volume 2

This material is based upon work supported by the
National Science Foundation
under Grant Numbers
ESI-9816320, REC-9806020, and RED-935373.

Any opinions, findings, and conclusions, or recommendations expressed in this material
are those of the author and do not necessarily reflect the views of the National Science Foundation.

 HOUGHTON MIFFLIN HARCOURT

Homework

Complete each division. Check your answer.

1. 5)4,820

2. 8)7,548

3. 9)7,535

4. 3)2,958

5. 7)5,857

6. 6)5,556

7. 7)6,945

8. 8)5,624

9. 4)3,254

Solve. Use estimation to check the solution.   *Show your work.*

10. Mrs. Wong drove between Chicago and St. Louis 8 times last month. Altogether she drove 2,376 miles. How far is it from Chicago to St. Louis?

_____

11. Jay has 6,200 beads. He is making bracelets with 9 beads each. How many bracelets can he make? How many beads will be left?

_____

12. There are 5,280 feet in a mile. There are 3 feet in a yard. How many yards are there in a mile?

_____

13. The Pencil Pal factory wraps pencils in packages of 6. Today there are 5,750 pencils to be packaged. How many packages will there be? How many pencils will be left over?

_____

Remembering

Write each fraction as a decimal.

1. $\frac{2}{10}$ _____

2. $\frac{556}{1,000}$ _____

3. $\frac{6}{100}$ _____

4. $\frac{17}{100}$ _____

5. $\frac{23}{1,000}$ _____

6. $\frac{5}{1,000}$ _____

7. $\frac{1}{10}$ _____

8. $\frac{33}{100}$ _____

9. $\frac{85}{100}$ _____

Solve.

10.
$$\begin{array}{r} 400 \\ \times\ 70 \\ \hline \end{array}$$

11.
$$\begin{array}{r} 300 \\ \times\ 30 \\ \hline \end{array}$$

12.
$$\begin{array}{r} 700 \\ \times\ 40 \\ \hline \end{array}$$

13.
$$\begin{array}{r} 20 \\ \times\ 50 \\ \hline \end{array}$$

14.
$$\begin{array}{r} 900 \\ \times\ 50 \\ \hline \end{array}$$

15.
$$\begin{array}{r} 800 \\ \times\ 30 \\ \hline \end{array}$$

Solve.

Show your work.

16. Sarah is dividing pies into eighths. She has 4 pies. How many eighths will she have?

_____

17. The track team plans to sprint 20 miles this school year. The runners will sprint $\frac{1}{4}$ mile each day. How many days will it take them to sprint 20 miles?

_____

18. **Stretch Your Thinking** Mrs. Thomas bought a bed for $1,548 and three armchairs. The bed cost 4 times as much as one armchair. How much did Mrs. Thomas spend altogether?

_____

           Divide Whole Numbers by One Digit

Homework

Divide.

1. $39\overline{)2,886}$

2. $81\overline{)7,533}$

3. $68\overline{)4,967}$

4. $72\overline{)4,968}$

5. $28\overline{)2,520}$

6. $33\overline{)1,287}$

7. $46\overline{)1,426}$

8. $55\overline{)990}$

Solve.

Show your work.

9. The lunchroom has enough seats for 168 students. Each class has 24 students. How many classes can eat in the lunchroom at the same time?

   _____

10. Mrs. Randall bought tickets to the art museum for all the fifth-grade students. Each ticket cost $12, and the total cost of the tickets was $1,152. How many fifth-grade students are there?

    _____

11. The Harmony Hotel has a total of 1,596 rooms. There are 42 rooms on each floor. How many floors does the Harmony Hotel have?

    _____

12. This year Martin earned $1,615 mowing lawns, shoveling driveways, and doing yardwork. This is 19 times as much as he earned last year. How much did Martin earn last year?

    _____

Explore Dividing by Two-Digit Whole Numbers **101**

Remembering

Solve. Use any method.   *Show your work.*

1.   68
   × 21

2.   36
   × 92

3.   25
   × 44

Complete each division. Check your answer.

4. 5)1,267

5. 3)1,374

6. 7)4,618

7. Chloe sorts her beads. The number of red beads she has is $5\frac{5}{6}$ times the number of green beads. If she has 60 green beads, how many red beads does she have?

_____

8. Brad plans to bike $15\frac{3}{4}$ miles. He has gone $\frac{2}{3}$ of the entire distance. How far has he gone?

_____

9. **Stretch Your Thinking** Write and solve a division problem that divides a 4-digit number by a 2-digit number. How did you estimate the first digit of the quotient?

_____

_____

Homework

Divide.

1. $34\overline{)7,276}$ 2. $85\overline{)6,120}$ 3. $73\overline{)4,309}$ 4. $38\overline{)3,576}$

5. $57\overline{)4,722}$ 6. $26\overline{)7,903}$ 7. $65\overline{)5,918}$ 8. $69\overline{)1,796}$

Solve.   *Show your work.*

9. A carousel factory has 1,252 carousel horses.
   48 horses are placed on each carousel. How
   many carousels can the factory build?

   _____

   How many horses will be left over?

   _____

10. Farmer Parson collected 1,183 chicken eggs this
    morning. He will put them in cartons that hold
    a dozen eggs each.

    How many cartons will he fill?

    _____

    How many eggs will be left over?

    _____

11. Write a division word problem using 7,903 and 26.

    _____

    _____

    _____

Remembering

Multiply. Simplify first if you can.

1. $\frac{3}{4} \cdot \frac{12}{13} =$ _____

2. $\frac{1}{4} \cdot \frac{3}{7} =$ _____

3. $\frac{7}{8} \cdot \frac{4}{5} =$ _____

4. $\frac{3}{8} \cdot \frac{4}{15} =$ _____

5. $\frac{4}{5} \cdot \frac{10}{12} =$ _____

6. $\frac{1}{5} \cdot \frac{5}{6} =$ _____

Complete the equations.

7. $0.65 \times 10^1 =$ _____

$0.65 \times 10^2 =$ _____

$0.65 \times 10^3 =$ _____

8. $0.8 \times 10^1 =$ _____

$0.8 \times 10^2 =$ _____

$0.8 \times 10^3 =$ _____

9. $2.45 \times 10^1 =$ _____

$2.45 \times 10^2 =$ _____

$2.45 \times 10^3 =$ _____

Divide.

10. $41\overline{)3,444}$

11. $36\overline{)1,944}$

12. $93\overline{)7,254}$

13. In Marla's school, $\frac{6}{15}$ of the students do not ride the bus to school. Of these students $\frac{5}{9}$ walk to school. What fraction of the students in Marla's school walk to school?

_____

14. **Stretch Your Thinking** Ben starts with a certain number of fruit chew packages. He puts 27 packages into each of 85 cases. He has 3 packages left. How many packages of fruit chews did Ben start with? Explain how you know.

_____

_____

_____

Too Large, Too Small, or Just Right?

Homework

Solve. Circle the choice that tells how you gave your answer.

Show your work.

1. A Ferris wheel holds 48 people. There are 823 people with tickets to ride the Ferris wheel. How many times will the Ferris wheel need to be run to give everyone a ride?

   whole number only   round up   mixed number   decimal   remainder only

2. Bananas cost 89 cents each at the fruit stand. Isabel has $11.75. How many bananas can she buy?

   whole number only   round up   mixed number   decimal   remainder only

3. The 15 members of a running club made $1,338 selling magazines. They will divide the money equally. How much should each runner get?

   whole number only   round up   mixed number   decimal   remainder only

4. There are 524 goldfish in the fish pond. They will be put in indoor tanks for the winter. If each tank holds 45 fish, how many tanks will be needed?

   whole number only   round up   mixed number   decimal   remainder only

5. Mr. Lopez made 339 ounces of strawberry jam. He plans to divide the jam equally among his 12 cousins. How many ounces of jam will each cousin get?

   whole number only   round up   mixed number   decimal   remainder only

Remembering

Compare. Write > (greater than) or < (less than).

1. 0.6 ◯ 0.06

2. 0.4 ◯ 0.41

3. 0.87 ◯ 0.8

4. 0.67 ◯ 0.76

5. 0.44 ◯ 0.39

6. 0.657 ◯ 0.668

Divide.

7. $66\overline{)5{,}745}$

8. $54\overline{)4{,}806}$

9. $36\overline{)2{,}597}$

Solve.

Show your work.

10. Martin asked friends to buy raffle tickets. On Saturday, he sold tickets to 5 of the 12 friends he asked. On Sunday, he sold tickets to 7 of the 9 friends he asked. On which day did he sell tickets to the greater fraction of the friends he asked?

_____

11. Emma bought $\frac{7}{8}$ yard of striped ribbon and $\frac{8}{9}$ yard of solid ribbon. Which kind of ribbon did she buy more of?

_____

12. **Stretch Your Thinking** Write and solve a division word problem for which the remainder is the answer.

_____

_____

_____

_____

Interpret Remainders

Homework

1. $7\overline{)3,990}$　　　　2. $44\overline{)2,156}$　　　　3. $5\overline{)7,003}$

4. $28\overline{)1,763}$　　　　5. $54\overline{)4,458}$　　　　6. $6\overline{)3,039}$

Solve.　　　　　　　　　　　　　　　　　　　　*Show your work.*

7. This morning, a factory produced 6,000 cans of beans and packaged them in boxes of 48 cans. How many boxes were filled?

   _____

8. Six friends earned $645 for painting some rooms in a neighbor's house. If they divide the money equally, how much will each friend get?

   _____

9. The floor of a ballroom has an area of 2,470 square feet. If the length of the floor is 65 feet, what is its width?

   _____

10. Felipe just started collecting stamps. He has 36 stamps so far. His uncle Carlo has 1,890 stamps in his collection. The number of stamps Carlo has is how many times the number Felipe has?

    _____

Remembering

Multiply.

1. 326
    × 2

2. 575
    × 5

3. 5,492
    × 8

4. 4,512
    × 9

5. 58
    × 43

6. 79
    × 52

7. 36
    × 21

8. 89
    × 67

Solve. Give your answer in simplest form.

9. $\frac{1}{8} \div 5 =$ _____

10. $\frac{1}{4} \cdot 1\frac{2}{3} =$ _____

11. $\frac{5}{6} - \frac{2}{3} =$ _____

12. $6 \div \frac{1}{3} =$ _____

13. $\frac{5}{6} + \frac{5}{8} =$ _____

14. $6\frac{3}{4} \cdot \frac{1}{6} =$ _____

Solve. Circle the choice that tells how you gave your answer.   *Show your work.*

15. A rollercoaster holds 45 people. There are 387 people waiting to board the rollercoaster. How many times will the rollercoaster need to run to give everyone a ride?

_____

whole number only   round up   mixed number   decimal   remainder only

16. **Stretch Your Thinking** I am a number less than 3,000. When you divide me by 32, my remainder is 30. When you divide me by 58, my remainder is 44. What number am I?

_____

Division Practice

Homework

Solve.

1. $9\overline{)6.57}$ 2. $5\overline{)36.41}$ 3. $4\overline{)9.584}$

4. $6\overline{)207.9}$ 5. $23\overline{)153.87}$ 6. $7\overline{)654.5}$

7. $45\overline{)431.1}$ 8. $2\overline{)7.006}$ 9. $16\overline{)5.76}$

Solve.   *Show your work.*

10. Teresa bought 16 roses for $20.64. How much did she pay for each rose?

11. Barry's dog Cubby is 1.26 meters long. Cubby is 7 times as long as Douglas's guinea pig Taffy. How long is Taffy?

12. Farmer Sanchez has 1,408.86 acres of land. He will divide it into 27 equal fields for spring planting. How many acres will be in each field?

13. Six friends will stay at a cabin in the woods this weekend. The distance to the cabin is 148.5 miles. Each person will drive one sixth of the distance. How far will each person drive?

Remembering

Solve.   *Show your work.*

1. Aiden buys a pair of jeans that costs $45.28. The sales tax that will be added to the cost of the jeans is $3.62. What is the total cost of the jeans?

   _____

2. When Madison got her kitten, Fluffy, he weighed 787.37 grams. He now weighs 2,085.8 grams more than he did when Madison first brought him home. How much does Fluffy weigh now?

   _____

Solve.

3.	150	4.	3.41	5.	2.28
	× 0.6		× 48		× 5

6.	0.9	7.	0.45	8.	0.03
	× 4		× 86		× 80

Divide.

9. 33)2,143   10. 9)4,140   11. 4)6,403

12. **Stretch Your Thinking** What part of this problem needs to be changed to make it correct? Explain how you know.
    $46 \div 8 = 6.75$

    _____

    _____

    _____

Name _____ **Date** _____

Homework

Solve.   *Show your work.*

1. Nella and Lydia are hiking 15 miles today. After every
   0.5 mile, they will stop and rest. How many times will
   they rest during the hike?

   _____

2. A cookie cutter shark is 0.4 meter long, and a thresher
   shark is 6 meters long. How many times as long as the
   cookie cutter shark is the thresher shark?

   _____

3. At a large wedding, the cakes were cut into hundredths,
   so each piece was 0.01 of a whole cake. If there were
   12 cakes, how many pieces were there?

   _____

4. A millimeter is 0.001 of a meter. How many millimeters
   are there in 7 meters?

   _____

5. Paco saves $0.75 each day for a new bicycle helmet.
   He has saved $36. For how many days has Paco been
   saving?

   _____

Solve.

6. $0.9\overline{)63}$ 7. $0.08\overline{)72}$ 8. $0.007\overline{)42}$ 9. $0.6\overline{)420}$

10. $0.4\overline{)372}$ 11. $0.6\overline{)534}$ 12. $0.26\overline{)884}$ 13. $0.71\overline{)1,136}$

Remembering

Solve.

Show your work.

1. Tyler is making a history project and needs two poster boards. He cuts one to measure 42.25 inches in length. He cuts the second to measure 34.75 inches in length. What is the difference between the two lengths of poster board?

_____

2. Ella has $2,251.88 in her bank account. She withdraws $852. How much money is left in her bank account?

_____

Solve.

3. $\begin{array}{r} 0.05 \\ \times\ 0.4 \\ \hline \end{array}$

4. $\begin{array}{r} 2.5 \\ \times\ 5 \\ \hline \end{array}$

5. $\begin{array}{r} 0.32 \\ \times\ 70 \\ \hline \end{array}$

6. $\begin{array}{r} 0.2 \\ \times\ 0.8 \\ \hline \end{array}$

7. $\begin{array}{r} 0.09 \\ \times\ 0.4 \\ \hline \end{array}$

8. $\begin{array}{r} 0.6 \\ \times\ 0.09 \\ \hline \end{array}$

Solve.

9. $5\overline{)17.4}$

10. $6\overline{)416.46}$

11. $7\overline{)32.55}$

12. **Stretch Your Thinking** Look at the division problem 112 ÷ 0.056. Without solving, how many zeros will be in the quotient? How do you know?

_____

_____

_____

Divide Whole Numbers by Decimal Numbers

Divide.

1. $0.07\overline{)4.2}$ **2.** $0.8\overline{)2.4}$ **3.** $0.05\overline{)4.8}$ **4.** $0.24\overline{)2.064}$

5. Circle the division that does *not* have the same answer as the others.

$54 \div 6$ $5.4 \div 0.6$ $0.54 \div 0.6$ $0.54 \div 0.06$ $0.054 \div 0.006$

Solve.   *Show your work.*

6. A beekeeper collected 7.6 liters of honey. She will pour it into bottles that each hold 0.95 liter. How many bottles will she fill?

_____

7. A very small dinosaur, the microraptor, was only 1.3 feet long. One of the largest dinosaurs, the diplodocus, was about 91 feet long. How many times as long as the microraptor was the diplodocus?

_____

8. Tomorrow, in the town of Eastwood, there will be a big race. The course is 5.25 kilometers long. A water station will be set up every 0.75 kilometer, including at the finish line. How many water stations will there be?

_____

9. Marisol's bedroom has an area of 29.76 square meters. The length of the room is 6.2 meters. What is its width?

_____

Remembering

Round to the nearest tenth.

1. 1.28 _____

2. 14.21 _____

3. 8.148 _____

Round to the nearest hundredth.

4. 4.769 _____

5. 45.124 _____

6. 16.107 _____

Solve.

7.   7.7
    × 1.4

8.   3.1
    × 0.05

9.   5.79
    × 0.9

10.   3.4
     × 8.8

11.   3.5
     × 0.46

12.   8.6
     × 0.90

Solve.

13. $0.9\overline{)36}$

14. $0.006\overline{)48}$

15. $0.04\overline{)32}$

16. $0.7\overline{)364}$

17. $0.34\overline{)2,210}$

18. $0.83\overline{)1,494}$

19. Stretch Your Thinking Must a decimal divisor and a decimal
dividend have the same number of decimal places in order
to have a whole-number quotient? Write a division equation
using two decimal numbers to support your answer.

_____

Homework

Divide.

1. $0.7\overline{)35}$ **2.** $0.06\overline{)24}$ **3.** $0.8\overline{)0.64}$ **4.** $0.03\overline{)18}$

5. $3\overline{)33}$ **6.** $0.05\overline{)0.65}$ **7.** $12\overline{)72}$ **8.** $0.04\overline{)11.56}$

9. $8\overline{)216}$ **10.** $0.8\overline{)490.4}$ **11.** $28\overline{)2,380}$ **12.** $0.033\overline{)5.148}$

Solve. Explain how you know your answer is reasonable.

Show your work.

13. Georgia works as a florist. She has 93 roses to arrange in vases. Each vase holds 6 roses. How many roses will Georgia have left over?

_____

_____

14. Julia is jarring peaches. She has 25.5 cups of peaches. Each jar holds 3 cups. How many jars will Julia need to hold all the peaches?

_____

_____

15. The area of a room is 114 square feet. The length of the room is 9.5 feet. What is the width of the room?

_____

_____

Remembering

Add or subtract.

1. $1\frac{1}{2}$
$+5\frac{5}{6}$

2. $2\frac{3}{5}$
$+5\frac{3}{10}$

3. $1\frac{1}{3}$
$-\frac{1}{6}$

4. $7\frac{3}{10}$
$+2\frac{1}{5}$

5. $9\frac{1}{8}$
$-2\frac{3}{4}$

6. 12
$-5\frac{2}{3}$

Find each product.

7. 7.8×1.2

8. 3.3×0.67

9. 91×0.49

10. 0.25×72

11. 68×0.17

12. 0.76×28

Divide.

13. $0.08\overline{)6.4}$

14. $0.8\overline{)7.2}$

15. $0.07\overline{)5.67}$

16. $0.58\overline{)5.336}$

17. $0.9\overline{)6.3}$

18. $0.05\overline{)1.75}$

19. **Stretch Your Thinking** Write a real world division problem for which you would drop the remainder.

_____

_____

_____

Homework

Multiply or divide.

1. $1.5 \times 5 =$ _____   **2.** $0.4 \times 0.05 =$ _____   **3.** $0.004 \times 0.03 =$ _____

4.   0.55
      $\times$ 0.07

5.   0.25
      $\times$ 0.12

6.   22.3
      $\times$ 6.2

7.   20.8
      $\times$ 0.26

8. $0.3\overline{)0.108}$ **9.** $0.11\overline{)407}$ **10.** $0.67\overline{)32.16}$ **11.** $0.44\overline{)105.6}$

For each problem, decide whether you need to multiply or divide. Then solve. Explain how you know your answer is reasonable.

Show your work.

12. Harriet makes yo-yos. She needs 38 inches of string for each yo-yo. How many yo-yos can she make with 875 inches of string? How many inches of string will be left over?

_____

_____

13. Roberto will save $\frac{1}{6}$ of his allowance each day. If he gets $2.00 a day, about how much money will he save each day? Round your answer to the nearest penny.

_____

_____

14. Raisins cost $0.97 per pound. Michael bought $15.52 worth of raisins. How many pounds of raisins did he buy?

_____

_____

© Houghton Mifflin Harcourt Publishing Company

Name _____ **Date** _____

Remembering

Multiply.

1. $\begin{array}{r} 47 \\ \times\ 7 \\ \hline \end{array}$

2. $\begin{array}{r} 181 \\ \times\ \ 3 \\ \hline \end{array}$

3. $\begin{array}{r} 4{,}609 \\ \times\ \ \ \ 5 \\ \hline \end{array}$

4. $\begin{array}{r} 2{,}115 \\ \times\ \ \ \ 6 \\ \hline \end{array}$

5. $\begin{array}{r} 86 \\ \times\ 75 \\ \hline \end{array}$

6. $\begin{array}{r} 22 \\ \times\ 15 \\ \hline \end{array}$

7. $\begin{array}{r} 53 \\ \times\ 25 \\ \hline \end{array}$

8. $\begin{array}{r} 38 \\ \times\ 36 \\ \hline \end{array}$

Divide.

9. $0.06\overline{)24}$

10. $0.3\overline{)228.6}$

11. $0.08\overline{)28.4}$

Tell whether you need to multiply or divide. Then solve.   *Show your work.*

12. A rectangle has an area of 4 square meters. The width is $\frac{1}{5}$ meter. What is the length of the rectangle?

_____

13. Audubon Preschool has 154 children in one age group. One seventh of those children arrive for early morning drop off. How many children arrive for early morning drop off?

_____

14. **Stretch Your Thinking** Write a division word problem that requires dividing two decimals to solve. Write a multiplication equation to check your answer.

_____

_____

_____

_____

Distinguish Between Multiplication and Division

Homework

Dividing numbers involves dividends, divisors, and quotients.

$$\text{divisor)}\overline{\text{dividend}}^{\text{quotient}}$$

Write a division problem (including the quotient) that satisfies all three statements.

Show your work.

1. The dividend is a one-digit whole number.
   The divisor is a one-digit whole number.
   The quotient is a one-digit whole number.

2. The dividend is a two-digit whole number.
   The divisor is a one-digit whole number.
   The quotient is a one-digit whole number.

3. The dividend is a two-digit whole number.
   The divisor is less than 1, and a number in tenths.
   The quotient is a two-digit whole number.

4. The dividend is a two-digit whole number.
   The divisor is greater than 1, and a number in tenths.
   The quotient is a two-digit whole number.

5. The dividend is a number in tenths.
   The divisor is a one-digit whole number.
   The quotient is a number in tenths.

6. The dividend is a decimal in hundredths.
   The divisor is a decimal in hundredths.
   The quotient is a one-digit whole number.

7. The dividend is a decimal in hundredths.
   The divisor is a decimal in hundredths.
   The quotient is a two-digit whole number.

Remembering

Add or subtract.

1. 21 + 1.08 = _____

2. 0.62 + 0.49 = _____

3. 0.06 + 0.5 = _____

4. 6 − 0.09 = _____

5. 3.01 − 0.8 = _____

6. 12.05 − 8 = _____

Complete each fraction box.

7.

$\frac{1}{3}$ and $\frac{4}{9}$	
>	
+	
−	
·	

8.

$\frac{2}{7}$ and $\frac{1}{4}$	
>	
+	
−	
·	

Multiply or divide.

9. 37.5
  × 3.5

10. 0.63
  × 0.27

11. $0.93\overline{)567.3}$

12. Stretch Your Thinking Use the term *dividend*, *divisor*, or *quotient* to complete each sentence. Then write a division equation that fits the description.

The _____ is a decimal in thousandths.

The _____ is a decimal in thousandths.

The _____ is a two-digit whole number.

Division problem: _____

Focus on Mathematical Practices

**Write an equation and use it to solve the problem.
Draw a model if you need to.**

1. Two professional baseball teams played a four-game series. Attendance for the first three games was 126,503 people, What was the Game 4 attendance if 171,318 people altogether attended the series?

Show your work.

_____

2. In the past, shares of stock were bought and sold in fractions of a dollar. Suppose one share of stock, purchased for $72\frac{1}{4}$ dollars per share, decreased in value to $66\frac{3}{8}$ dollars per share. What was the decrease in value per share?

_____

3. Two shipping containers are being loaded into the cargo hold of a ship. One container weighs 2.3 tons. What is the weight of the other container if the total weight of both containers is 4.15 tons?

_____

4. The heights of horses are often measured in units called hands. Abigail's pony is $13\frac{1}{4}$ hands tall. How much taller is Jermaine's horse if it is $16\frac{1}{2}$ hands tall?

_____

5. Jake plays baseball with two wooden bats—one made from hickory and one made from white ash. What is the weight of his white ash bat if his hickory bat weighs 32.4 ounces, and both bats together weigh 64.33 ounces?

_____

6. Seventeen fewer people attended the second basketball game of the season than attended the first game. One hundred ninety-two people attended the second game. How many people attended the first game?

_____

Remembering

Add or subtract.

1. $4\frac{1}{8} + 1\frac{5}{8} =$

2. $4\frac{3}{5} + 6\frac{1}{5} =$

3. $6\frac{2}{3} - 5\frac{1}{3} =$

4. $7 - 1\frac{1}{2} =$

5. $8\frac{3}{4} - 2\frac{3}{4} =$

6. $\frac{2}{7} + \frac{4}{7} =$

7. $\begin{array}{r} 15 \\ -\ 3\frac{1}{7} \\ \hline \end{array}$

8. $\begin{array}{r} 5\frac{4}{5} \\ +\ 1\frac{1}{8} \\ \hline \end{array}$

9. $\begin{array}{r} 11\frac{1}{5} \\ -\ 9\frac{3}{4} \\ \hline \end{array}$

10. $\begin{array}{r} 1\frac{5}{6} \\ +\ \frac{1}{3} \\ \hline \end{array}$

11. $\begin{array}{r} 2\frac{2}{3} \\ +\ 7\frac{5}{9} \\ \hline \end{array}$

12. $\begin{array}{r} 6\frac{3}{7} \\ +\ 1\frac{1}{14} \\ \hline \end{array}$

Copy each exercise. Then subtract.

13. $12{,}389 - 2.75 =$

14. $165.98 - 127.2 =$

15. $326.55 - 23.81 =$

16. Stretch Your Thinking Garrett wants to buy a new soccer ball, a pair of shorts, and a pair of soccer shoes. The ball costs $12.55, the shorts cost $22.98, and the shoes cost $54.35. Garrett has $85.00. How much more money does Garrett need? Write an equation to solve the problem.

_____

_____

Situation and Solution Equations for Addition and Subtraction

Solve each problem. Draw a model if you need to.

Show your work.

1. Spectators for a high school football game sit in bleachers along one side of the field. Altogether, the bleachers seat 1,152 spectators in 16 rows of equal length. How many spectators can be seated in one row of the bleachers?

   _____

2. How many periods of time, each $\frac{1}{3}$ of an hour long, does a 8-hour period of time represent?

   _____

3. The area of a rectangular ceiling is 130.5 square feet, and one measure of the ceiling is 14.5 feet. What is the other measure of the ceiling?

   _____

4. Sorbet is a frozen dessert that is often made from fruit. How many portions, each weighing $\frac{1}{10}$ of a kilogram, can a French dessert chef create from 3 kilograms of sorbet?

   _____

5. The family room floor in Zack's home has a rectangular area rug that measures 6.5 feet by 9 feet. The floor is rectangular and measures 10 feet by 12 feet. What area of the floor is not covered by the rug?

   _____

6. A cargo van is carrying 20 identical steel cylinders. Each cylinder contains compressed oxygen. Altogether, the cylinders weigh $\frac{1}{2}$ of a ton.

   a. In tons, what is the weight of each cylinder?

   _____

   b. One ton = 2,000 pounds. In pounds, what is the weight of each cylinder?

   _____

Remembering

Multiply.

1. $\frac{6}{7} \cdot 42 =$ _____

2. $\frac{1}{3} \cdot 36 =$ _____

3. $\frac{4}{5} \cdot 15 =$ _____

4. $\frac{1}{4} \cdot 28 =$ _____

5. $\frac{5}{9} \cdot 81 =$ _____

6. $\frac{3}{8} \cdot 72 =$ _____

Write an equation. Then solve.

Show your work.

7. There is $\frac{1}{4}$ of a peach pie left after a family picnic. Four cousins share the leftover pie equally. What fraction of a whole pie will each cousin receive?

_____

8. Tully has 24 stamps in his collection. This is $\frac{1}{3}$ times the number Jordan has. How many stamps does Jordan have?

_____

Write an equation to solve the problem. Draw a model if you need to.

9. Candace jumped 11.45 feet in a long jump competition. What is the length of Maria's jump if she jumped 1.05 fewer feet than Candace?

_____

10. **Stretch Your Thinking** Ms. Jackson has $97.00 to spend on games for her classroom. She buys six board games that cost $11.95 each and a video game that costs $24.10. How much money does Ms. Jackson have left to buy more games? Write an equation to solve the problem.

_____

_____

Situation and Solution Equations for Multiplication and Division

Homework

Write a word problem for the equation.
Draw a model to show the product.

Show your work.

1. $\frac{2}{3} \cdot 3 = \frac{6}{3}$

_____

_____

_____

_____

2. $\frac{3}{4} \cdot \frac{1}{2} = \frac{3}{8}$

_____

_____

_____

_____

3. $2 \div \frac{1}{4} = 8$

_____

_____

_____

_____

Name _____   **Date** _____

Remembering

Complete each fraction box.

1.

$\frac{3}{4}$ and $\frac{5}{6}$	
>	
+	
−	
·	

2.

$\frac{3}{5}$ and $\frac{8}{15}$	
>	
+	
−	
·	

Solve.

Show your work.

3. A $1,508 award is shared equally by 8 people. What is each person's share of the award?

_____

4. Felipe has 54 coins in his collection. His brother Pedro has 1,269 coins. The number of coins Pedro has is how many times the number his brother has?

_____

Write an equation to solve the problem. Draw a model if you need to.

5. How many periods of time, each $\frac{1}{6}$ of an hour long, does a 10-hour period of time represent?

_____

6. Stretch Your Thinking Write a word problem for the following equation. $\frac{4}{5} \cdot \frac{1}{4} + \frac{3}{5} = \frac{4}{5}$

_____

_____

_____

_____

Write Word Problems

Homework

Write an equation to solve the problem. Use mental math or estimation to show that your answer is reasonable.

Show your work.

1. In a speed test, a computer took 12.4 seconds to complete one task, and 37.8 seconds to complete a more difficult task. How much time was needed to complete both tasks?

   Equation: _____

   Estimate: _____

   _____

2. To walk to school, Pablo first walks $\frac{1}{2}$ kilometer to Tanya's house. Then Pablo and Tanya walk $\frac{3}{5}$ kilometer to school. How far does Pablo walk to school?

   Equation: _____

   Estimate: _____

   _____

3. Each Saturday morning, Andy works 4 hours and earns $34. At that rate, what does Andy earn for each hour he works?

   Equation: _____

   Estimate: _____

   _____

4. Yuri completed a race in 0.88 fewer seconds than Josie. Josie's time was 23.95 seconds. How long did it take Yuri to complete the race?

   Equation: _____

   Estimate: _____

   _____

   _____

Name _____ Date _____

Remembering

Write an estimated answer for each problem. Then find and write each exact answer.

Estimated Answer	Exact Answer

1. $41 \times 77 \approx$ _____ $\times$ _____ $\approx$ _____ $41 \times 77 =$ _____

2. $3.8 \times 1.9 \approx$ _____ $\times$ _____ $\approx$ _____ $3.8 \times 1.9 =$ _____

3. $7.3 \times 5.01 \approx$ _____ $\times$ _____ $\approx$ _____ $7.3 \times 5.01 =$ _____

Divide.

4. $45\overline{)6,733}$ 5. $61\overline{)7,892}$ 6. $28\overline{)3,123}$

Write a word problem for the equation. Draw a model to show the product.

7. $\frac{5}{6} \cdot 4 = \frac{20}{6}$

_____

_____

_____

_____

8. **Stretch Your Thinking** Kaley has $2\frac{3}{8}$ yards of fabric. She cuts and uses $1\frac{1}{16}$ yards from the fabric. She estimates that less than 1 yard of fabric is left over. Is her estimate reasonable? Explain.

_____

_____

_____

Determine Reasonable Answers

Homework

Solve each problem.   *Show your work.*

1. Michael has 21 T-shirts. One third of them are blue. How many of Michael's T-shirts are blue?

   _____

2. There are 476,092 fish in the city aquarium. That number of fish is 476,070 more fish than Nadia has in her aquarium. How many fish does Nadia have in her aquarium?

   _____

3. Anne-Marie has saved 9 dollars for a new coat. That is $\frac{1}{6}$ as much money as she needs. How much does the coat cost?

   _____

4. Last year it rained on 63 days in Mudville. There were 7 times as many days of rain in Mudville as in Desert Hills. How many days did it rain in Desert Hills last year?

   _____

5. Maria wants to buy a new car. She will choose a green car or a silver car. The green car costs $16,898, and the silver car costs $1,059.75 less than the green car. What is the cost of the silver car?

   _____

6. At a country-music concert, 48 people played guitars. That number is 6 times as many as the number of people who played banjos. How many people at the concert played banjos?

   _____

7. There are 8 apples left on the table. There are $\frac{1}{4}$ as many apples as bananas left on the table. How many bananas are there?

   _____

Name _____ **Date** _____

Remembering

Add or subtract.

1. $6\frac{6}{7}$
   $+ 2\frac{3}{14}$

2. $1\frac{2}{3}$
   $- \frac{5}{9}$

3. $12\frac{4}{5}$
   $- 8\frac{5}{10}$

4. 11
   $- 5\frac{5}{11}$

5. $7\frac{1}{5}$
   $+ 1\frac{2}{3}$

6. $9\frac{3}{4}$
   $+ 2\frac{5}{6}$

7. Use the number line to find $\frac{2}{3} \cdot \frac{4}{5}$.

   Label all the parts above and below. _____

   0 |————————————————————————————| 1

Write an equation to solve the problem. Use mental math or estimation to show that your answer is reasonable.

8. Terrell runs two timed drills at practice. The first drill takes 33.5 seconds and the second drill takes 28.2 seconds. How much time does it take him to complete both drills?

   Equation: _____

   Estimate: _____

   _____

   _____

9. **Stretch Your Thinking** Maverick has a $12\frac{3}{4}$-foot-long streamer to decorate a hallway at his school. He cuts off $\frac{3}{8}$ of a foot from each end to make it fit the hallway. His principal asks him to make another streamer that is $\frac{5}{6}$ as long. How long is the new streamer?

   _____

Language of Comparison Problems

Homework

Solve. Draw a model if you will find it helpful.

1. A flagpole flying the Ohio state flag is $\frac{9}{10}$ the height of a 30-foot-tall flagpole that is flying the U.S. flag. What is the height (*h*) in feet of the flagpole flying the Ohio state flag?

   _____

2. The number of students in the Period 7 study hall at Jin's school is 4 times the number of students in Jin's home room. How many students (*s*) are in the study hall if there are 16 students in Jin's home room?

   _____

3. The enrollment at Roosevelt High School is 1,045 students, which is 5 times the enrollment of Truman Middle School. How many students (*s*) are enrolled at Truman Middle School?

   _____

4. A truck weighs 5,400 pounds. An open-wheel race car weighs $\frac{1}{4}$ as much. How much does the race car weigh?

   _____

5. Owen and Maya each studied for a test. Owen studied for 90 minutes and Maya studied for 0.5 times that length of time. Who studied more? Multiply to check your prediction.

   Prediction: _____

6. Sonia's family has 2 children, which is $\frac{2}{3}$ the number of children in Zeke's family. Which family has more children? Divide to check your prediction.

   Prediction: _____

Remembering

Copy each exercise. Then add or subtract

1. $22.09 - 17 =$ _____   **2.** $7 - 0.05 =$ _____   **3.** $4.07 - 0.3 =$ _____

4. $44 + 5.06 =$ _____   **5.** $0.07 + 0.8 =$ _____   **6.** $0.55 + 0.31 =$ _____

Solve.

7. $0.5 \times 0.04 =$ _____   **8.** $0.3 \times 0.7 =$ _____   **9.** $0.07 \times 0.2 =$ _____

10. $\begin{array}{r} 0.46 \\ \underline{\times\ 80} \end{array}$ **11.** $\begin{array}{r} 0.06 \\ \underline{\times\ 0.8} \end{array}$ **12.** $\begin{array}{r} 3.2 \\ \underline{\times\ 9} \end{array}$

Solve each problem.   *Show your work.*

13. A soccer team has 35 soccer balls. One fifth of the balls are made of leather. How many of the balls are leather?

_____

14. There are 5 fifth graders who play basketball. That is 7 times the number of fifth graders who play tennis. How many fifth graders play tennis?

_____

15. Stretch Your Thinking Samantha draws a hopscotch diagram on the sidewalk in front of her house. The diagram is 10 feet long. Her neighbor asks her to draw a 4-foot hopscotch diagram on a canvas mat. In simplest form, what fraction of the length of Samantha's diagram is her neighbor's diagram?

_____

Multiplicative Comparison Problems

Homework

Write an equation and use it to solve the problem. Draw a model it you need to.

Show your work.

1. The Yukon River is 1,980 miles long, and twice as long as the Platte River. How many miles long (*l*) is the Platte River?

   _____

2. The height of the Empire State Building in New York City is 1,250 feet, and 364 fewer feet than the height of the World Financial Center building in Shanghai, China. What is the height (*h*) of the World Financial Center building?

   _____

3. Olivia is 48 inches tall, and $\frac{2}{3}$ as tall as her brother Cameron. In inches, how tall (*t*) is Cameron?

   _____

4. Sydney is shopping for a new television. The cost of a 32-inch LCD flat screen is $149.95. The cost of 46-inch LED flat screen is $280.04 more. What is the cost (*c*) of the 46-inch LED flat screen television?

   _____

5. After arriving home from school, Luis read for $\frac{1}{3}$ of an hour. If he reads for $1\frac{1}{6}$ hours after dinner, how many hours (*h*) will Luis have read altogether?

   _____

6. Each morning, Jared needs 60 minutes to get ready for school. Kiara needs $\frac{7}{12}$ as much time as Jared. How many minutes does Kiara need each morning to get ready for school?

   _____

7. When compared to Tasha, Liam spent 20 additional minutes doing homework. Liam took 45 minutes to complete his homework. How long did it take Tasha?

   _____

Remembering

Solve.

1.	6.9	2.	7.3	3.	5.8
	× 4.2		× 0.90		× 0.54

4.	5.3	5.	0.7	6.	9.4
	× 0.08		× 6.25		× 1.7

Divide.

7. $0.05\overline{)4.5}$

8. $0.3\overline{)1.5}$

9. $0.04\overline{)2.32}$

10. $0.64\overline{)4.928}$

11. $0.6\overline{)5.43}$

12. $0.08\overline{)4.32}$

Solve. Draw a model if you will find it helpful.

13. The gymnasium at Audubon Middle School is $\frac{5}{6}$ the height of a 30-foot-tall building that is next to the gymnasium. What is the height (h) in feet of the gymnasium?

_____

14. Amiee's karate instructor has 595 students. That is 5 times the number of students that her dance instructor has. How many students does her dance instructor have?

_____

15. **Stretch Your Thinking** Draw a model that shows $5 \cdot \frac{3}{5} = 3$.

_____

Types of Comparison Problems

Name _____ **Date** _____

Homework

Solve each problem if possible. If a problem does not
have enough information, write the information that is
needed to solve the problem.

Show your work.

1. At the school bookstore, Quinn purchased a binder
   for $4.75 and 4 pens for $0.79 each. What was
   Quinn's total cost (c)?

   _____

2. A school bus has 12 rows of seats, and 4 students can be
   seated in each row. How many students (s) are riding the
   bus if 11 rows are filled with students, and 2 students are
   riding in the twelfth row?

   _____

3. A group of 16 friends visited an amusement park. When
   they arrived, $\frac{3}{4}$ of the friends wanted to ride the fastest
   roller coaster first. How many friends (f) wanted to ride?

   _____

4. Zeke is shipping clerk for a large business. Today he
   spent 90 minutes preparing boxes for shipping. One box
   weighed 10 pounds and 7 boxes each weighed $3\frac{1}{2}$ pounds.
   What is the total weight (w) of the boxes?

   _____

5. A middle school faculty parking lot has 3 rows of parking
   spaces with 13 spaces in each row, and 1 row of 7 spaces.
   How many vehicles (v) can be parked in the faculty lot?

   _____

6. Rochelle's homework always consists of worksheets. Last
   night, the average amount of time she needed to complete
   each worksheet was 15 minutes. How much time (t) did
   Rochelle spend completing worksheets last night?

   _____

Remembering

Multiply.

1. 56	2. 256	3. 3,801	4. 4,239
× 3	× 7	× 6	× 9

5. 84	6. 67	7. 88	8. 42
× 23	× 18	× 39	× 45

Multiply or divide.

9. $0.67\overline{)502.5}$ 10. $0.21\overline{)945}$ 11. 0.55 × 0.30   12. 32.5 × 6.3

**Write an equation and use it to solve the problem.
Draw a model it you need to.**

13. Lindsay is shopping for a new CD player. The cost of one CD player she is considering is $56.55. The cost of a higher priced CD player is $14.25 more. What is the cost (c) of the higher priced CD player?

_____

14. **Stretch Your Thinking** Use the equation below to write a word problem. Leave out one piece of information that is needed to solve the problem and describe the information that should have been included. $b = (5 \cdot 6) + 10$

_____
_____
_____
_____

Equations and Parentheses

Name _____   **Date** _____

Homework

Solve each problem.   *Show your work.*

1. After a deposit of $100, a withdrawal of $125, and a deposit
   of $24, the balance in a savings account was $27.28. What
   was the balance (*b*) before the deposits and withdrawal?

   _____

2. The charge for a plumbing repair was $29.60 for parts,
   $1\frac{1}{4}$ hours for labor at $56 per hour, and a $40 for the
   service call. What was the total cost (*c*) of the repair?

   _____

3. Ebi, Jose, Derell, and Asami measured their heights. Ebi's
   height was 2.5 cm greater than Jose's height. Jose's height
   was 3.1 cm greater than Derell's height. Derell's height was
   0.4 cm less than Asami's height. Ebi is 162.5 cm tall. How
   tall (*t*) is Asami?

   _____

4. A school bus has 22 rows of seats, and 4 students can be
   seated in each row. Students riding in the bus have filled
   19 rows of seats, and $\frac{1}{2}$ of the remaining seats. How many
   seats on the bus are empty (*e*)?

   _____

5. Rosa is 13 years and 6 months old and her brother Malcolm
   is 11 years and 6 months old. Their great grandfather is
   89 years old. How many years (*y*) older is the great grandfather
   than the combined ages of Rosa and Malcolm?

   _____

6. A riverfront business offers raft trips. The capacity of each
   raft is 4 people. Suppose 29 adults and 22 children would
   like to raft. If each raft is filled to capacity, how many
   people (*p*) will be aboard the last raft?

   _____

Remembering

Solve.

1. 500
   × 60

2. 500
   × 50

3. 900
   × 40

4. 30
   × 10

5. 200
   × 70

6. 300
   × 80

Complete each division. Check your answer.

7. $7\overline{)3,451}$

8. $4\overline{)2,155}$

9. $8\overline{)4,122}$

10. $5\overline{)1,242}$

11. $3\overline{)2,114}$

12. $9\overline{)5,778}$

Write and solve an equation to solve the problem. If the problem does not have enough information, write the information that is needed to solve the problem.

13. Danny has $14.75, Jason has $22.10, and Trey has $87.45. How much more money (m) does Trey have than the combined amounts of the other two boys?

Show your work.

_____

14. **Stretch Your Thinking** Write a multistep word problem in which the remainder is the solution. Write an equation that will solve it.

_____
_____
_____
_____

Multistep Word Problems

Solve each problem.   *Show your work.*

1. A savings account balance was $135.10 before a withdrawal of $60, a deposit of $22.50, and a withdrawal of $45. What was the balance *(b)* after the withdrawals and deposit?

   _____

2. The charge for a bicycle repair was $9.28 for parts, $\frac{1}{4}$ hour of labor at $18 per hour, and a $2 shop fee. What was the total cost *(c)* of the repair?

   _____

3. While shopping at the school bookstore, Ric purchased 4 book covers for $1.25 each, and a pen that cost $\frac{2}{5}$ as much as a book cover. What amount of change *(c)* did Ric receive if he paid for his purchase with a $10 bill?

   _____

4. A junior baseball team plays 16 games each summer. Last summer the team scored an average of 3.25 runs per game during the first half of the season. The team scored a total of 29 runs during the second half of the season. How many runs *(r)* were scored by the team last season?

   _____

5. Four family members compared their ages. Terell is 3 years younger than Danny. Danny is 1 year younger than Pablo. Pablo's age is $\frac{1}{3}$ Shaniqua's age. How old is Terell *(t)* if Shaniqua is 36 years old?

   _____

6. Twenty-four soccer players, four coaches, and one equipment manager are traveling to a game in minivans. The capacity each minivan is 6 people. How many people *(p)* are riding in the last minivan if the other minivans are filled to capacity?

   _____

Name _____ **Date** _____

Remembering

Multiply.

1. 495
   × 7

2. 126
   × 6

3. 2,689
   × 3

4. 3,249
   × 8

5. 78
   × 21

6. 68
   × 55

7. 41
   × 33

8. 92
   × 89

Divide.

9. $0.7\overline{)49}$

10. $0.03\overline{)18}$

11. $0.4\overline{)0.8}$

12. $0.09\overline{)27}$

13. $0.5\overline{)172.5}$

14. $0.06\overline{)8.4}$

Write an equation to solve the problem.

15. After a deposit of $250, a withdrawal of $312, and a deposit of $15, the balance in a savings account is $67.50. What was the balance (b) before the deposits and withdrawal?

_____

16. **Stretch Your Thinking** Write an equation that is represented by the following diagram.

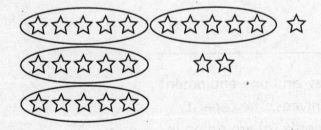

_____

Practice Problem Solving

Homework

The data below represent typical weights for five different breeds of adult male dogs. Make a bar graph to display the data. Choose an appropriate scale based on the weights of the dogs.

Type of Dog	Adult Weight (in pounds)
Labrador retriever	65.25
German shepherd	$75\frac{1}{4}$
golden retriever	72.8
boxer	$70\frac{1}{2}$
standard poodle	64.3

Remembering

Compare. Write > (greater than) or < (less than).

1. 0.05 ◯ 0.5   2. 0.61 ◯ 0.6   3. 0.77 ◯ 0.7

4. 0.34 ◯ 0.43   5. 0.28 ◯ 0.29   6. 0.981 ◯ 0.978

Solve the problem.

7. The charge for skating is $6.35 for skate rental, $1\frac{1}{3}$ hours
   of skating at $18 per hour, and an additional $1 fee.
   What is the total cost (c) for skating?

   _____

8. **Stretch Your Thinking** Make a table that lists the
   data from the bar graph.

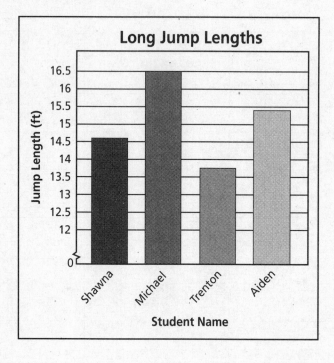

Homework

1. Consider the expression $2\frac{1}{2} - (\frac{3}{4} + \frac{5}{8})$.

   a. Which operation is done first, subtraction or addition?

   _____

   b. Write the computation in words.

   _____

2. Consider the expression $4.5 + 6 \times 0.1$.

   a. Which operation is done first, addition or multiplication?

   _____

   b. Write the computation in words.

   _____

Write the computation in words.

3. $7 \div \frac{1}{7}$ _____

4. $8 - t$ _____

5. $3.6 \div 0.4 - 0.5$ _____

6. $5 \cdot (6 + 7)$ _____

Write an expression for the words.

7. Add $\frac{1}{6}$ and $\frac{4}{9}$. _____

8. Subtract the product of 5 and 11 from 100. _____

9. Divide 9 by 2 and then add 5.7. _____

10. Multiply 42 by the sum of 4 and r. _____

Name
Date

Remembering

Complete each division. Check your answer.

1. $3\overline{)1,957}$
2. $9\overline{)3,103}$
3. $7\overline{)5,768}$

Divide.

4. $69\overline{)4,899}$
5. $87\overline{)2,001}$
6. $52\overline{)3,432}$

7. $25\overline{)1,175}$
8. $38\overline{)2,660}$
9. $46\overline{)2,438}$

Write an equation to solve the problem. Draw a model if you need to.

10. Jesse drives $6\frac{3}{8}$ miles in a golf cart during a round of golf. Payton drives $7\frac{3}{4}$ miles. How much farther does Payton drive?

_____

11. Stretch Your Thinking Write the computation in words for an expression that uses all four operations (addition, subtraction, multiplication, and division). Then, write an expression for the words.

_____

_____

_____

Read and Write Expressions

Homework

1. Follow the Order of Operations to simplify $27 \div (3 \cdot 3) + 17$

   Step 1 Perform operations inside _____
   parentheses.

   Step 2 Multiply and divide from left _____
   to right.

   Step 3 Add and subtract from left to _____
   right.

Simplify. Follow the Order of Operations.

2. $54 - 200 \div 4$

3. $0.8 \div (0.07 - 0.06)$

4. $3 \cdot 8 - 6 \div 2$

5. $(\frac{3}{8} + \frac{1}{4}) \cdot 16$

6. $64 + 46 - 21 + 29$

7. $72 \div (7 - 1) \cdot 3$

8. $0.8 - 0.5 \div 5 + 0.2$

9. $\frac{5}{6} - 4 \cdot \frac{1}{12}$

10. $5 \cdot 15 \div 3$

11. $32 \div (2.3 + 1.7) \cdot 3$

12. $(1\frac{1}{2} - \frac{3}{4}) \times \frac{1}{4}$

13. $(6.3 - 5.1) \cdot (0.7 + 0.3)$

14. $12 \div 0.1 + 12 \div 0.01$

15. $\frac{1}{2} \cdot \frac{1}{2} \div \frac{1}{2}$

16. $10 - 4 + 2 - 1$

Remembering

Solve.

1. $5\overline{)44.3}$ **2.** $2\overline{)125.65}$ **3.** $5\overline{)34.565}$

Write an equation to solve the problem. Draw a model if you need to.

4. The students of Turner Middle School are going on a field trip. There are 540 students attending. A bus can hold 45 students. How many buses are needed for the field trip?

_____

5. The area of a rectangular court is 433.37 square meters, and the length of the court is 28.7 meters. What is width of the court?

_____

Write the computation in words.

6. $5 \div \frac{1}{8}$ _____

7. $2.4 \div 0.6 + 0.2$ _____

8. Stretch Your Thinking Write step-by-step instructions for simplifying the following expression.

$$10 \cdot [60 \div (11 + 4)] - 3$$

_____

_____

_____

_____

Simplify Expressions

Homework

Evaluate the expression.

1. $m \div 0.3$ for $m = 1.8$ 2. $3\frac{1}{3} - x$ for $x = \frac{5}{6}$ 3. $50 - n \div 2$ for $n = 30$

4. $x \cdot 1\frac{1}{2}$ for $x = 10$ 5. $10 \cdot (20 + d)$ for $d = 30$ 6. $120 \div (x \cdot 6)$ for $x = 2$

7. $a \cdot \frac{1}{3} + 3 \div \frac{1}{3}$ for $a = 3$ 8. $(0.15 - t) \cdot 100$ for $t = 0.02$ 9. $h \div 0.07$ for $h = 4.9$

10. Max bought a pair of jeans for $32 and three T-shirts for
    t dollars each.

    a. Write an expression for the total amount Max spent.

    _____

    b. If each T-shirt cost $9, how much did Max spend?

    _____

11. Luke is 4 years younger then Zoe. Mischa is half Luke's age.
    Let z be Zoe's age.

    a. Write an expression for Luke's age.

    _____

    b. Write an expression for Mischa's age.

    _____

    c. If Zoe is 16 years old, how old are Luke and Mischa?

    _____

Remembering

Solve.

1. $0.8\overline{)64}$

2. $0.008\overline{)72}$

3. $0.04\overline{)16}$

4. $0.5\overline{)80}$

5. $0.48\overline{)1,536}$

6. $0.76\overline{)1,596}$

Write a word problem for the equation. Draw a model to show the product.

7. $\frac{1}{2} \cdot \frac{4}{5} = x$

_____

_____

_____

_____

_____

Simplify. Follow the Order of Operations.

8. $\frac{3}{5} - 2 \cdot \frac{1}{10}$

9. $40 \div (6 - 1) \cdot 3$

10. $\left(\frac{1}{2} + \frac{3}{8}\right) \cdot 24$

11. $0.4 \div (0.09 - 0.07)$

12. $66 - 150 \div 10$

13. $6 \cdot 5 - 9 \div 3$

14. Stretch Your Thinking Write a two-operation expression
that equals 31 when evaluated for $x = 5$.

_____

Simplify Expressions

Homework

1. a. Write the first five terms of a numerical pattern that begins with 2 and then adds 3.

   _____

   b. Write an expression for the sixth term of the pattern.

   _____

   c. Write the sixth term.

   _____

2. a. Write the first five terms of a pattern that begins with 5, and then adds 5.   ___ ___ ___ ___ ___

   b. Write the first five terms of a pattern that begins with 20, and then adds 20.   ___ ___ ___ ___ ___

   c. Circle the corresponding pairs of terms in the patterns. How does the top term compare to the bottom term?

   _____

   d. How does the bottom term compare to the top term?

   _____

Complete the table and use it for Problems 3 and 4.

Cost of Music Downloads

Number of Songs	1	2	3	4	5
Cost in Dollars	$0.99	$1.98			

3. Describe a relationship shared by the corresponding terms.

   _____

   _____

4. What would be the cost of downloading 6 songs?

   _____

Remembering

Solve.   *Show your work.*

1. Manny has 40 ounces of butter that he is cutting into
   1.25-ounce slices. How many slices will he have?

   _____

2. Tracy is running in a 5.25-kilometer race on Saturday.
   A marathon is approximately 42 kilometers. How many
   times as long as Tracy's race is a marathon?

   _____

**Write an equation to solve the problem. Use mental math
or estimation to show that your answer is reasonable.**

3. Each Saturday morning, Janie works 5 hours and
   earns $35.75. How much does Janie earn for each
   hour she works?

   Equation: _____

   Estimate: _____

   _____

Evaluate the expression.

4. $120 \div (t \cdot 3)$ for $t = 4$ 5. $m \cdot 2\frac{2}{3}$ for $m = 5$ 6. $4 \cdot (2 + c)$ for $c = 8$

7. $7\frac{1}{2} - p$ for $p = \frac{5}{6}$ 8. $60 - z \div 2$ for $z = 20$ 9. $x \div 0.9$ for $x = 3.6$

10. **Stretch Your Thinking** Create your own numerical pattern.
    Write the starting number, the rule, and the first 5 terms in
    the pattern. Then write an expression for the tenth term.

    _____

    _____

Use the coordinate plane below to answer the questions.

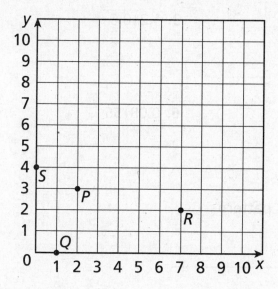

Write an ordered pair to represent the location of each point.

1. point P _____   **2.** point Q _____   **3.** point R _____   **4.** point S _____

Plot and label a point at each location.

5. point W at (3, 9)   **6.** point X at (3, 5)   **7.** point Y at (9, 5)

Solve.

8. Suppose points W, X, and Y represent three vertices of rectangle WXYZ. Where should point Z be plotted?

_____

Plot and label point Z. Then use a ruler to draw the rectangle.

9. What ordered pair represents the point at the center of the rectangle?

_____

10. Use subtraction to find the lengths of segments WX and XY. Show your work.

_____

Name _____   **Date** _____

Remembering

Divide.

1. $0.9\overline{)54}$

2. $0.09\overline{)27}$

3. $1.2\overline{)0.6}$

4. $0.06\overline{)48}$

5. $0.4\overline{)188.4}$

6. $0.08\overline{)56}$

7. **a.** Write the first five terms of a numerical pattern that begins with 5 and then adds 6.

_____

b. Write an expression for the sixth term of the pattern.

_____

c. Write the sixth term.

_____

8. Stretch Your Thinking List and graph four ordered pairs that are vertices of a rectangle with a perimeter of 16 units.

_____

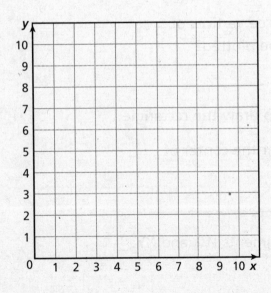

The Coordinate Plane

Homework

The *add 3* table below shows a numerical pattern in the left column and the result of adding 3 in the right column.

add 3	
0	3
1	
2	
3	
4	

(x, y)
(____, ____)
(____, ____)
(____, ____)
(____, ____)
(____, ____)

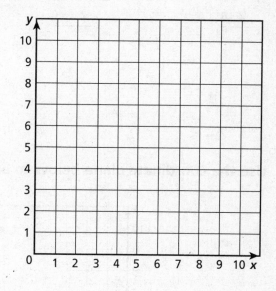

1. Complete the *add 3* table.

2. Complete the (x, y) table.

3. Each (x, y) pair of terms represents a point. Graph and connect the points.

A freight train is traveling at a constant speed of 20 miles per hour.

4. Complete the table to show the distance the train will travel in 0, 1, 2, and 3 hours.

Time (hr)	0	1	2	3
Distance (mi)		20		

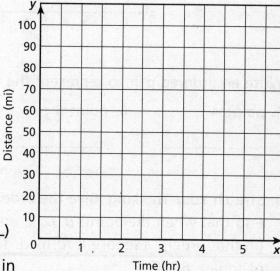

5. Write the ordered (x, y) pairs the data represent. Then graph and connect the points and extend the line.

(____, ____) (____, ____) (____, ____) (____, ____)

6. How far would you expect the train to travel in $2\frac{1}{2}$ hours? Explain your answer.

_____

_____

Name _____ **Date** _____

Remembering

Multiply.

1. 76
   × 4

2. 199
   × 6

3. 7,907
   × 2

4. 98
   × 78

Use the coordinate plane below to answer the questions.

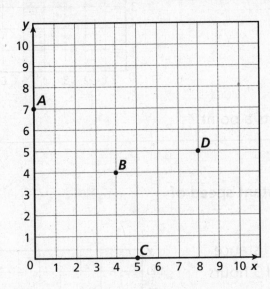

Write an ordered pair to represent the location of each point.

5. point A

6. point B

7. point C

8. point D

_____   _____   _____   _____

9. **Stretch Your Thinking** Give the ordered pair for a point
   E so that when the points B, D, E, and C are connected
   (in that order), a square is formed. Then, find the area
   of square BDEC.

   _____

Graph Ordered Pairs

Name _____ **Date** _____

Homework

1. On the coordinate plane below, plot and label points to design your own constellation. When you return to class, share your constellation with your class.

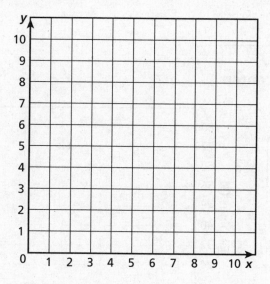

2. Write the name of your constellation.

_____

3. Write the order in which your points are to be connected.

_____

_____

_____

4. Explain how you can tell that two points will be on the same horizontal line just by looking at their coordinates.

_____

_____

5. Explain how you can tell that two points will be on the same vertical line just by looking at their coordinates.

_____

_____

Remembering

Write and solve an equation to solve the problem.

1. A group of 25 classmates visits an amusement park. When they arrive, $\frac{3}{5}$ of the students want to ride the fastest roller coaster first. How many students is this?

_____

Nicole makes $8 per hour working at a daycare center.

2. Complete the table.

Time (hr)	0	1	2	3
Earnings ($)		8		

3. Write the ordered (x, y) pairs the data represent. Then graph and connect the points and extend the line.

_____, _____, _____, _____

4. How much money would Nicole make in $2\frac{1}{2}$ hours? Explain your answer.

_____

_____

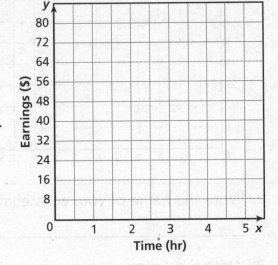

5. **Stretch Your Thinking** Which points listed lie on the line? Which points do not lie on the line? Explain.

(0, 5) (1, 5) (2, 4), (3, 6), (4, 3)

_____

_____

_____

_____

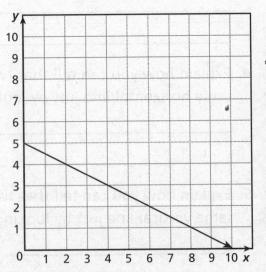

Focus on Mathematical Practices

Homework

Complete.

1. 75 cm = _____ m

2. 802 cm = _____ m

3. 251 km = 251,000 _____

4. 0.95 mm = _____ cm

5. 0.46 cm = _____ mm

6. 32 m = _____ mm

7. 58 mm = _____ m

8. 2,581 m = _____ km

9. 35.6 mm = _____ cm

10. 2.92 cm = 29.2 _____

Solve.

11. Jason ran 325 meters farther than Kim ran. Kim ran
    4.2 kilometers. How many meters did Jason run? Estimate
    to check your answer.

    _____

    Estimate: _____

12. On each of 3 days, Derrick rode 6.45 km to school,
    150 meters to the library, and then 500 meters back home.
    How many kilometers did he ride for the 3 days altogether?

    _____

13. Lisa wants to frame her little brother's drawing as a gift to
    her mother. The rectangular drawing is 43.5 centimeters
    by 934 millimeters. How many centimeters of wood
    framing will she need?

    _____

14. Marguerite is building a box from strips of wood. She needs
    78 pieces of wood that are each 29 centimeters long. The
    wood comes in boards that are 6 meters long. How many
    boards will she need? Explain.

    _____

    _____

    _____

Remembering

Multiply.

1. 89
   × 7

2. 221
   × 3

3. 6,077
   × 6

4. 77
   × 65

Suppose a plant grows at the rate shown in the table.
Use the table to complete Exercises 5 and 6.

Growth of a Plant	
Age (weeks)	Height (cm)
0	0
1	10
2	20
3	30
4	40

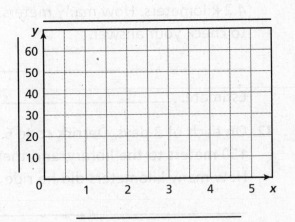

5. Write five ordered pairs that the data represent.

6. Graph the ordered pairs. What does each axis of the
   graph represent? Title the graph and label each axis.

7. **Stretch Your Thinking** Find the sum of 130 cm and
   50 mm in meters. Show your work.

Homework

Complete.

1. 5,811 mL = _____ L

2. 297 L = _____ kL

3. 1.09 kL = 1,090 _____

4. 32,500 mL = _____ L

5. 53.1 L = _____ mL

6. 5.66 L = _____ mL

7. 2,848 mL = _____ L

8. 431 L = _____ kL

9. 0.56 L = _____ mL

10. 0.78 L = 780 _____

Solve.

11. Jennifer made 5 L of punch for her party. Her brother made another 750 mL. If they combine the two batches, how many 180 mL servings would they have? Would there be any punch left over? If so, how much?

    _____

12. On an average day, a horse might drink 50 L, a sheep might drink 4 L, and a chicken might drink 200 mL. How much water would a farm with 3 horses, 15 sheep, and 12 chickens need for a day?

    _____

13. Terrell has a water purifier for backpacking. It will purify 1 liter of water in 1 minute. How long would it take Terrell to purify enough water for 4 canteens that each hold 750 mL, and two that each hold 1.5 L?

    _____

14. The Institute of Medicine determined that a man should drink 3 liters of fluids a day and a woman should drink 2.2 liters. Mr. Morrison drank 880 mL of water at breakfast and Mrs. Morrison drank 700 mL. How much more will they both need to drink combined to meet the recommended amounts for the day?

    _____

Name _____   **Date** _____

Remembering

Suppose the cost of sugar changes at the rate shown in the table. Use the table to complete Exercises 1 and 2.

Cost of Sugar	
Weight (lb)	Cost ($)
0	$0
1	$1.40
2	$2.80
3	$4.20
4	$5.60

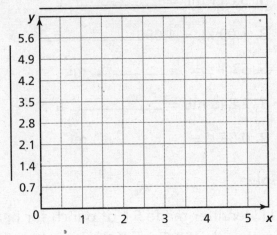

1. Write five ordered pairs that the data represent.

_____

2. Graph the ordered pairs. What does each axis of the graph represent? Title the graph and label each axis.

_____

_____

Complete the equation.

3. 14 m = _____ mm

4. 0.35 mm = _____ cm

5. 790 cm = _____ m

6. 0.88 cm = _____ mm

7. 782 km = 782,000 _____

8. 58 cm = _____ m

9. **Stretch Your Thinking** Shannon pours four different liquid ingredients into a bowl. The sum of the liquid ingredients is 8.53 liters. Two of her measurements are in liters and two of her measurements are in milliliters. Give an example of possible measurements for Shannon's four liquids.

_____

_____

Metric Units of Liquid Volume

Homework

Complete.

1. 973 mg = 0.973 _____

2. 0.058 g = 58 _____

3. 10.64 kg = _____ g

4. 4.001 kg = _____ mg

5. 29 g = 0.029 _____

6. 7 mg = _____ g

7. 3.7 g = _____ mg

8. 84 g = _____ kg

Solve.

9. The mass of substances left in a sample after the liquid is evaporated is called the *total dissolved solids*. Kim split up 2 liters of water into three different samples and boiled all the liquid away in each. The masses of solids left in the three samples were 2.025 grams, 457 mg, and 589 mg. Using the table at the right, how should Kim classify the water?

Total Dissolved Solids in 1 Liter of Solution	
fresh	< 1,000 mg
brackish	1,000 to 10,000 mg
saline	> 10,000 mg

_____

10. Jamal watched his older brother Robert lift weights. The bar alone had a mass of 20 kg. On the bar he had two 11.4 kg weights, two 4.5 kg weights, and four 450 g weights. What mass was Robert lifting?

_____

11. Barry bought 25 kg of fish-flavored cat food and 35 kg of chicken-flavored cat food for the cat rescue center. He is going to divide the cat food into packets of 300 grams. How many packets will he make?

_____

Remembering

Greyson rides his bike at a constant rate. In 30 minutes, Greyson can bike 7 miles.

1. Complete the table to show the distance Greyson can ride in 0, 30, 60, and 90 minutes.

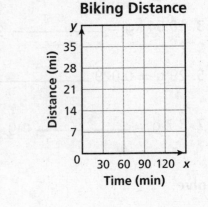

Biking Distance

Time (min)	0	30	60	90
Distance (mi)		7		

2. Write the ordered (x, y) pairs the data represent. Then graph the points and extend the line.

(___, ___) (___, ___) (___, ___) (___, ___)

3. How far would you expect Greyson to ride in 105 minutes? Explain your answer.

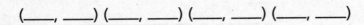

_____

_____

Complete the equation.

4. 435 L = _____ kL

5. 6.71 L = _____ mL

6. 86,300 mL = _____ L

7. 109 L = _____ kL

8. 5,669 mL = _____ L

9. 30.8 L = _____ mL

10. 9.12 kL = 9,120 _____

11. 9,235 mL = _____ L

12. **Stretch Your Thinking** Write three measurements using grams and three measurements using milligrams that total 15.4 grams.

_____

_____

Metric Units of Mass

Homework

Complete.

1. 36 in. = _____ ft

2. 12 ft = _____ yd

3. 36 in. = _____ yd

4. _____ in. = 4 ft

5. _____ ft = 2 yd

6. _____ in. = 3 yd

7. _____ ft = 90 in.

8. _____ in. = $5\frac{1}{2}$ ft

9. 6 yd = _____ in.

10. _____ yd = 432 in.

11. $1\frac{1}{4}$ yd = _____ ft

12. 90 ft = _____ yd

Find the perimeter of each figure in feet.

13.

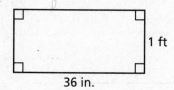

36 in.
1 ft

P = _____

14.

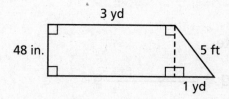

3 yd
48 in.
5 ft
1 yd

P = _____

Find the perimeter of each figure in yards.

15.

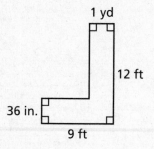

1 yd
12 ft
36 in.
9 ft

P = _____

16.

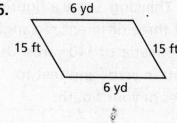

6 yd
15 ft
15 ft
6 yd

P = _____

Remembering

Write an expression for the words.

1. Multiply 12 by the sum of 8 and t. _____

2. Divide 10 by 4 and then subtract 6.2. _____

3. Add the product of 7 and 10 to 80. _____

4. Subtract $\frac{1}{8}$ from $\frac{5}{6}$. _____

Simplify. Follow the Order of Operations.

5. $12 - 7 + 9 - 2$ **6.** $15 \div 0.3 + 6 \div 0.02$ **7.** $(2\frac{3}{8} - \frac{1}{4}) \times \frac{1}{5}$

8. $\frac{1}{6} \cdot \frac{1}{6} \div \frac{1}{6}$ **9.** $(7.2 - 3.3) \cdot (0.5 + 0.5)$ **10.** $36 \div (6.6 + 2.4) \cdot 4$

Complete.

11. 5 mg = _____ g

12. 13.45 kg = _____ g

13. 66 g = 0.066 _____

14. 0.021 g = 21 _____

15. 5.003 kg = _____ mg

16. 782 mg = 0.782 _____

17. Stretch Your Thinking Draw a figure composed of three different rectangles that has a perimeter of 140 yards. Use measurements in yards and feet to label the sides of your figure.

_____

Name _____ **Date** _____

Homework

Complete.

1. 2 pt = _____ qt

2. 4 qt = _____ gal

3. 2 c = _____ pt

4. 3 qt = _____ pt

5. 1 qt = _____ c

6. 5 gal = _____ qt

7. _____ qt = 52 c

8. _____ qt = 46 pt

9. 112 c = _____ gal

10. $11\frac{1}{2}$ gal = _____ qt

11. 112 c = _____ pt

12. 75 pt = _____ qt

Write a fraction.

13. What fraction of 1 gallon is 1 quart?

_____

14. What fraction of 1 quart is 3 cups?

_____

15. What fraction of 1 gallon is 5 cups?

_____

16. What fraction of 1 pint is 1 cup?

_____

Solve.

Show your work.

17. Cesar bought 2 bottles of juice that each hold 2 quarts and another bottle that holds $1\frac{1}{2}$ gallons of juice. How many quarts of juice did he buy?

_____

18. Samantha saw two bottles of ketchup at the store for the same price. One bottle contained 4 pints of ketchup, and the other contained 1.25 quarts of ketchup. Which bottle was the better bargain?

_____

19. A pitcher is full of lemonade. Which unit of liquid volume best describes the amount of lemonade in the pitcher? Explain.

_____

_____

_____

Remembering

Divide.

1. $5\overline{)2{,}245}$ 2. $6\overline{)3{,}277}$ 3. $9\overline{)4{,}558}$

4. $56\overline{)1{,}344}$ 5. $47\overline{)3{,}619}$ 6. $23\overline{)2{,}047}$

7. $91\overline{)4{,}315}$ 8. $62\overline{)4{,}030}$ 9. $18\overline{)1{,}241}$

Complete.

10. 24 in. = _____ ft   11. 27 ft = _____ yd   12. 3 ft = _____ in.

13. _____ in. = 5 yd   14. _____ yd = 18 ft   15. _____ ft = 84 in.

16. 24 yd = _____ ft   17. 8 ft = _____ in.   18. _____ ft = 84 yd

19. **Stretch Your Thinking** What fraction of a gallon
    is 3 pints?

_____

Name _____ **Date** _____

Homework

Complete.

1. 1 lb = _____ oz

2. 2 T = _____ lb

3. 32 oz = _____ lb

4. 1,000 lb = _____ T

5. 4 lb = _____ oz

6. 10,000 lb = _____ T

Write a mixed number in simplest form to represent the number of pounds equivalent to each number of ounces.

7. 40 oz = _____ lb

8. 50 oz = _____ lb

9. 44 oz = _____ lb

10. 68 oz = _____ lb

11. 22 oz = _____ lb

12. 94 oz = _____ lb

Solve.

Show your work.

13. At a garden center, grass seed sells for $8 per pound. Kalil spent $10 on grass seed. What amount of seed did he buy?

_____

14. Two boxes of tea weigh 3 oz. The Tea Time Tasty Tea Company packs 112 boxes in a case of tea. How many pounds does each case of tea weigh?

_____

15. Juli uses 12 ounces of cheese in her potato soup recipe. Her recipe yields 8 servings. If Juli needs enough for 20 servings, how many pounds of cheese will she need?

_____

16. At a grocery store, salted peanuts in the shell cost 30¢ per ounce. Is $5.00 enough money to buy 1 pound of peanuts? If it is, what amount of money will be left over?

_____

Remembering

Complete the pattern.

1. $5 \times 10^1 = 5 \times 10 =$ _____

$5 \times 10^2 = 5 \times 100 =$ _____

$5 \times 10^3 = 5 \times 1,000 =$ _____

$5 \times 10^4 = 5 \times 10,000 =$ _____

2. $45 \times 10^1 =$ _____ $= 450$

$45 \times 10^2 =$ _____ $= 4,500$

$45 \times 10^3 =$ _____ $= 45,000$

$45 \times 10^4 =$ _____ $= 450,000$

3. $17 \times 10^1 = 17 \times 10 =$ _____

$17 \times 10^2 = 17 \times 100 =$ _____

.$17 \times 10^3 = 17 \times 1,000 =$ _____

$17 \times 10^4 = 17 \times 10,000 =$ _____

4. $342 \times 10^1 =$ _____ $= 3,420$

$342 \times 10^2 = 342 \times 100 =$ _____

$342 \times 10^3 =$ _____ $= 342,000$

$342 \times 10^4 = 342 \times 10,000 =$ _____

Solve.

5. 8 qt = _____ pt

6. 2 qt = _____ c

7. _____ c = 2 pt

8. 80 cups = _____ gal

9. $9\frac{1}{2}$ gal = _____ qt

10. 80 cups = _____ pt

11. _____ qt = 24 cups

12. _____ pt = 32 qt

13. _____ qt = 25 pt

14. Stretch Your Thinking Divide 15 pounds of rice into four unequal measures using ounces.

_____

Homework

1. Perry is growing maple saplings. After 3 weeks, he measured the saplings to the nearest quarter inch and drew this line plot with the data. Use the line plot to answer questions about the saplings.

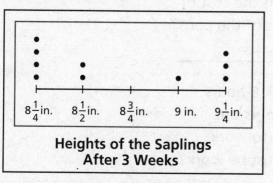

Heights of the Saplings After 3 Weeks

a. How many saplings were there?

_____

b. How many saplings were less than 9 inches tall?

_____

c. What is the combined height of all the saplings?

_____

2. As a volunteer at the animal shelter, Uma weighed all the puppies. She made a list of the weights as she weighed them. The puppies weights were $3\frac{3}{4}$ lb, $4\frac{1}{4}$ lb, $3\frac{1}{2}$ lb, $3\frac{3}{4}$ lb, $3\frac{1}{4}$ lb, $3\frac{3}{4}$ lb, $3\frac{1}{2}$ lb, $4\frac{1}{4}$ lb, and $3\frac{3}{4}$ lb.

a. Draw a line plot of the puppies' weights.

b. Use the line plot to write and answer a question about the data.

_____

_____

_____

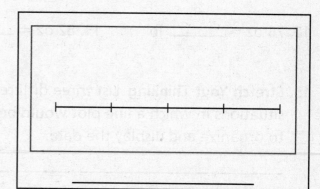

Remembering

Write an equation to solve each problem. *Show your work.*

1. At the school bookstore, Harrison purchases 3 notebooks for $2.50 each, 10 pens for $0.35 each, and 5 mechanical pencils for $0.89 each. By what amount (*a*) is the cost of the mechanical pencils greater than the cost of the pens?

   _____

2. This week an employee is scheduled to work 6 hours each day Monday through Friday, and $3\frac{1}{2}$ hours on Saturday morning. If the employee's goal is to work 40 hours, how many additional hours (*h*) must he work?

   _____

Complete.

3. 6 T = _____ lb

4. 3 lb = _____ oz

5. _____ oz = 5 lb

6. 5,000 lb = _____ T

7. 8 lb = _____ oz

8. 20,000 lb = _____ T

Write a mixed number in simplest form to represent the number of pounds equivalent to each number of ounces.

9. 66 oz = _____ lb

10. 52 oz = _____ lb

11. 24 oz = _____ lb

12. 76 oz = _____ lb

13. 82 oz = _____ lb

14. 46 oz = _____ lb

15. **Stretch Your Thinking** List three different real world situations in which a line plot would be the best choice to organize and display the data.

   _____

   _____

   _____

   _____

Read and Make Line Plots

Homework

Find the perimeter and the area of the rectangle.

1.

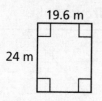

19.6 m

24 m

$P =$ _____

$A =$ _____

2.

$43\frac{5}{12}$ ft

11 ft

$P =$ _____

$A =$ _____

Find the side length of the rectangle.

3.

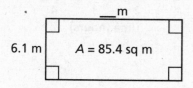

____ m

6.1 m $A = 85.4$ sq m

4.

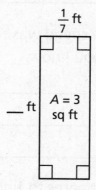

$\frac{1}{7}$ ft

____ ft $A = 3$ sq ft

5.

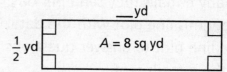

____ cm

0.4 cm $A = 5.68$ sq cm

6.

____ yd

$\frac{1}{2}$ yd $A = 8$ sq yd

Solve.

7. Gerard ran out of tile for his patio. The width of the remaining area is $2\frac{2}{9}$ feet. The length of the remaining area is 7 feet. How much does Gerard have left to tile?

_____

8. Kyra is building a dollhouse. The carpet for the bedroom is 27 square inches. The length of the bedroom is 6 inches. How long is the width?

_____

Remembering

The graph shown represents a skier traveling at a constant speed.

1. The points on the graph represent four
   ordered (*x, y*) pairs. Write the ordered pairs.

   (____, ____) (____, ____) (____, ____) (____, ____)

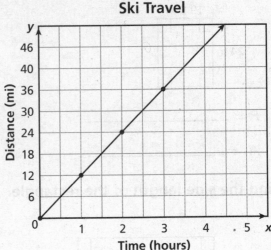

Ski Travel

2. Complete the table to show the relationship
   that time and distance share.

Time (hours)	0			
Distance (miles)	0			

3. At what constant rate of speed was the skier
   traveling? Explain how you know.

   _____

   _____

   _____

4. Dayna surveyed her classmates to find out
   how many e-mails they send per day. Then,
   she drew this line plot with the data.
   Use the line plot to answer questions
   about the e-mails sent.

   a. How many classmates were surveyed?

   _____

   b. How many classmates sent fewer than
      5 e-mails?

   _____

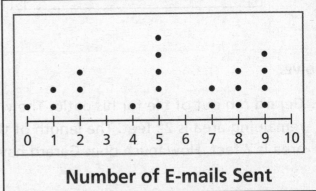

Number of E-mails Sent

   c. How many classmates sent at least 7 e-mails?

   _____

5. **Stretch Your Thinking** Find the fractional side lengths of a rectangle
   that has a perimeter of $64\frac{5}{6}$ inches. Then find the area of the rectangle.

   _____

Perimeter and Area of Rectangles

Homework

1. Alison had a box in the shape of a cube. She decided to use centimeter cubes to find the volume of the box. It took 75 centimeter cubes to fill the box with no gaps. What was the volume of the box?

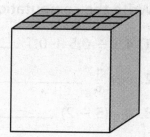

_____

Find the number of unit cubes and the volume.

2.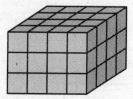

Number of unit cubes: _____

Volume: _____

3.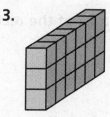

Number of unit cubes: _____

Volume: _____

4.

Number of unit cubes: _____

Volume: _____

5.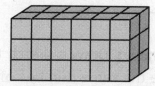

Number of unit cubes: _____

Volume: _____

6.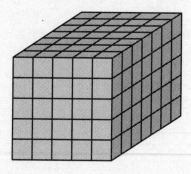

Number of unit cubes: _____

Volume: _____

7.

Number of unit cubes: _____

Volume: _____

Remembering

Write the computation in words.

1. $4.5 \div 0.5 + 0.1$ _____

2. $6 \div \frac{1}{6}$ _____

3. $4 \cdot (5 - 2)$ _____

4. $11 - c$ _____

Find the perimeter and the area of the rectangle.

5.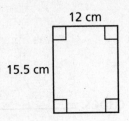

12 cm

15.5 cm

$P =$ _____

$A =$ _____

6.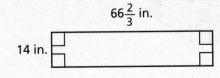

$66\frac{2}{3}$ in.

14 in.

$P =$ _____

$A =$ _____

7. **Stretch Your Thinking** Draw a sketch to show two
   figures that have the same number of unit cubes
   that look different from each other.

Homework

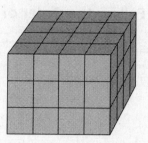

Use the prism on the right to answer the questions.

1. How many cubes are in 1 layer? _____

2. How many layers are in the prism? _____

3. Write a multiplication expression for the volume.

   _____

4. What is the volume of the prism? _____

Find the volume.

5.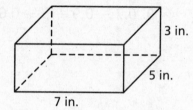

   3 in.

   5 in.

   7 in.

   Volume: _____

6.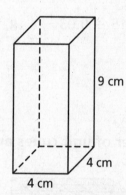

   9 cm

   4 cm

   4 cm

   Volume: _____

7.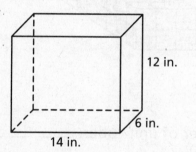

   12 in.

   6 in.

   14 in.

   Volume: _____

8.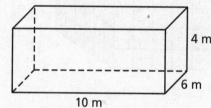

   4 m

   6 m

   10 m

   Volume: _____

9.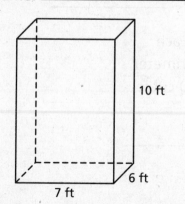

   10 ft

   6 ft

   7 ft

   Volume: _____

10.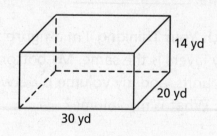

    14 yd

    20 yd

    30 yd

    Volume: _____

Name _____ **Date** _____

Remembering

Solve. Follow the Order of Operations.

1. $21 - 6 + 3 - 6$

2. $(7.9 - 5.1) \cdot (0.2 + 0.8)$

3. $6 \cdot 10 \div 5$

4. $\frac{1}{5} \cdot \frac{1}{5} \div \frac{1}{5}$

5. $(2\frac{3}{8} - \frac{1}{4}) \times \frac{1}{8}$

6. $\frac{5}{8} - 3 \cdot \frac{1}{16}$

7. $16 \div 0.2 + 15 \div 0.03$

8. $64 \div (6.6 + 1.4) \cdot 2$

9. $0.7 - 0.9 \div 3 + 0.6$

Find the number of unit cubes and the volume.

10.

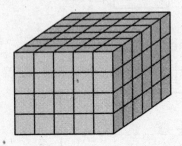

11.

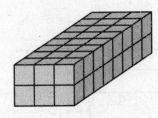

Number of unit cubes: _____

Number of unit cubes: _____

Volume: _____

Volume: _____

12. Stretch Your Thinking I'm a figure with six layers. Each of my layers is the same. My bottom layer has a perimeter of 28 units, and my volume is between 200 and 300 cubic units. What is my volume?

_____

Visualize Volume

Name _____ **Date** _____

Homework

Write a numerical expression for the volume. Then calculate the volume.

1.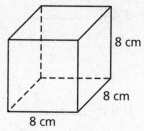
8 cm
8 cm
8 cm

2.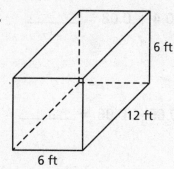
6 ft
12 ft
6 ft

3.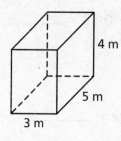
4 m
5 m
3 m

Expression: _____

Volume: _____

Expression: _____

Volume: _____

Expression: _____

Volume: _____

Find the unknown dimension or volume of each rectangular prism.

4. V = _____

   l = 4 cm

   w = 4 cm

   h = 11 cm

5. V = 168 cu yd

   l = _____

   w = 7 yd

   h = 3 yd

6. V = 90 cu in.

   l = 9 in.

   w = _____

   h = 5 in.

Write an equation. Then solve.

7. Pattie built a rectangular prism with cubes. The base of her prism has 12 centimeter cubes. If her prism was built with 108 centimeter cubes, how many layers does her prism have?

_____

8. Isabella cares for an aquarium that is 6 feet long and has a height of 4 feet. The aquarium needs 72 cubic feet of water to be completely filled. What is the width of the aquarium?

_____

9. Ray's aquarium is 20 inches long, 20 inches wide, and has a height of 15 inches. Randal's aquarium is 40 inches long, 12 inches wide, and has a height of 12 inches. Whose aquarium has a greater volume? By how much?

_____

Remembering

Add or subtract.

1. $0.45 + 0.77 =$ _____

2. $0.4 + 0.08 =$ _____

3. $6.9 - 3.44 =$ _____

4. $7 - 2.2 =$ _____

5. $0.66 + 0.96 =$ _____

6. $5.7 - 0.9 =$ _____

Find the volume.

7.

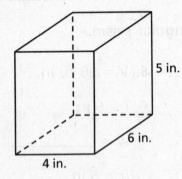

Volume: _____

8.

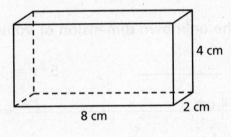

Volume: _____

9. Stretch Your Thinking Give the dimensions of a crate that could be used to ship 6 of the boxes below. Allow for some air space between the boxes so they can fit in the crate.

_____

_____

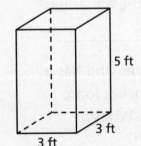

Introduce Volume Formulas

Homework

For each question, write whether you would measure for length, area, or volume.

1. the amount of space inside a moving van _____

2. the number of tiles needed to cover a bathroom

   floor _____

3. the distance from a porch to a tree _____

4. the amount of water a tank holds _____

5. the height of a flagpole _____

Solve.

6. A box is 5 inches long, 4 inches wide, and 1 inch deep. How much space is inside the box?

   _____

7. Aponi built a toy chest for her niece. It has a volume of 12 cubic feet. The chest is 3 feet long and 2 feet wide. How deep is it?

   _____

8. The rug in Alan's room has an area of 18 square feet. He is planning to buy another rug that is twice as long and twice as wide. What is the area of the new rug?

   _____

9. Each drawer in Monique's nightstand has a volume of 6 cubic decimeters. Each drawer in her dresser is twice as long, twice as wide, and twice as deep. What is the volume of one of Monique's dresser drawers?

   _____

10. Fong and Daphne built these structures. Who used more cubes? How many more?

    _____

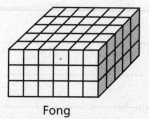

Fong

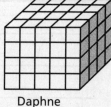

Daphne

Remembering

Solve.

1.	3.8	2.	0.30	3.	3.3
	× 5.4		× 6.7		× 0.78

4.	0.04	5.	0.6	6.	8.3
	× 7.3		× 5.14		× 2.8

Find the unknown dimension or volume of each rectangular prism.

7. $V = $ _____

$l = 7$ cm

$w = 4$ cm

$h = 9$ cm

8. $V = 200$ cu yd

$l = $ _____

$w = 5$ yd

$h = 5$ yd

9. $V = 160$ cu in.

$l = 10$ in.

$w = $ _____

$h = 4$ in.

10. $V = $ _____

$l = 10$ cm

$w = 8$ cm

$h = 6$ cm

11. $V = 297$ cu m

$l = $ _____

$w = 9$ m

$h = 3$ m

12. $V = 126$ cu in.

$l = 9$ in.

$w = $ _____

$h = 7$ in.

13. **Stretch Your Thinking** Give one real world example for measuring each of the following: perimeter, area, volume.

_____

_____

_____

_____

Name _____ **Date** _____

Homework

Find the volume of each composite solid figure.

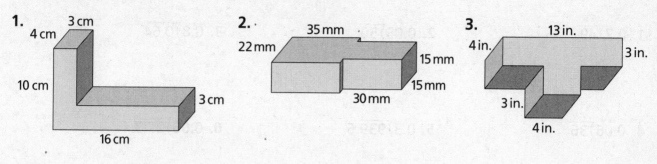

1. 3 cm
4 cm
10 cm
3 cm
16 cm

_____

2. 35 mm
22 mm
15 mm
15 mm
30 mm

_____

3. 13 in.
4 in.
3 in.
3 in.
4 in.

_____

4. The exterior of a refrigerator is shaped like a rectangular prism, and measures $2\frac{2}{3}$ feet wide by $5\frac{1}{2}$ feet high by $2\frac{1}{2}$ feet deep. What amount of space does the refrigerator take up?

_____

5. In the space below, draw a composite solid of your own design that is made up of two prisms. Write the dimensions of your design, and then calculate its volume.

Name _____   **Date** _____

Remembering

Divide

1. $0.7\overline{)49}$

2. $0.05\overline{)50}$

3. $0.8\overline{)0.64}$

4. $0.06\overline{)36}$

5. $0.3\overline{)939.6}$

6. $0.06\overline{)27.3}$

Solve.

7. A fish tank is 20 feet long, 12 feet wide, and 10 feet deep. What is the volume of the fish tank?

_____

8. Stretch Your Thinking Draw a composite solid in the space below using two different rectangular prisms. Label the length and width using fractions of units. The figures do not need to be to scale. Find the volume of the figure.

_____

Volume of Composite Solid Figures

Homework

Circle all the names that describe the shape.

1.

quadrilateral   trapezoid

parallelogram   rhombus

rectangle   square

2.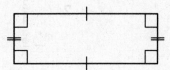

quadrilateral   trapezoid

parallelogram   rhombus

rectangle   square

3.

quadrilateral   trapezoid

parallelogram   rhombus

rectangle   square

4.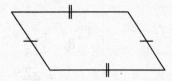

quadrilateral   trapezoid

parallelogram   rhombus

rectangle   square

Sketch a shape that fits the description, if possible.

5. a trapezoid with two right angles

6. a rhombus with a line of symmetry

7. a parallelogram with a right angle that is not a rectangle

8. a rectangle with opposite sides that are not congruent

Name _____   **Date** _____

Remembering

Add or subtract.

1. $\dfrac{5}{6}$
    $-\dfrac{1}{3}$

2. $\dfrac{3}{4}$
    $-\dfrac{5}{8}$

3. $\dfrac{3}{16}$
    $-\dfrac{1}{8}$

4. $\dfrac{5}{9}$
    $+\dfrac{1}{3}$

5. $\dfrac{3}{5}$
    $+\dfrac{1}{4}$

6. $\dfrac{1}{6}$
    $+\dfrac{2}{3}$

7. 6
    $-3\dfrac{2}{5}$

8. $1\dfrac{4}{9}$
    $+4\dfrac{2}{3}$

9. $6\dfrac{4}{5}$
    $-2\dfrac{1}{10}$

Find the volume of each composite solid.

10.

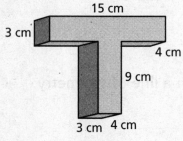

15 cm
3 cm
4 cm
9 cm
3 cm   4 cm

_____

11.

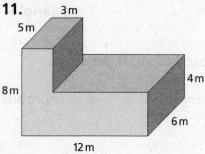

3 m
5 m
8 m
4 m
6 m
12 m

_____

12.

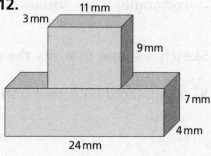

3 mm
11 mm
9 mm
7 mm
4 mm
24 mm

_____

13. **Stretch Your Thinking** Explain why a square is always a rectangle but a rectangle is not always a square.

_____

_____

_____

_____

Attributes of Quadrilaterals

Homework

Circle all the names that describe the shape.

1.

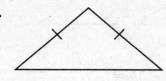

acute	scalene
right	isosceles
obtuse	equilateral

2.

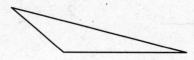

acute	scalene
right	isosceles
obtuse	equilateral

3.

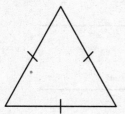

acute	scalene
right	isosceles
obtuse	equilateral

4.

acute	scalene
right	isosceles
obtuse	equilateral

Sketch a shape that fits the description, if possible.

5. a triangle with two obtuse angles

6. a right scalene triangle

7. an acute triangle that is not equilateral

8. a scalene triangle with a line of symmetry

Name _____ **Date** _____

Remembering

Solve.

1. $\frac{1}{5} \div 6 =$ _____

2. $7 \div \frac{1}{4} =$ _____

3. $\frac{6}{7} \cdot \frac{1}{5} =$ _____

4. $\frac{1}{10} \div 5 =$ _____

5. $4 \cdot \frac{1}{5} =$ _____

6. $\frac{1}{3} \cdot 14 =$ _____

Find each product by first rewriting each mixed number as a fraction.

7. $\frac{3}{5} \cdot 1\frac{1}{6} =$ _____

8. $2\frac{2}{3} \cdot 6 =$ _____

9. $4\frac{5}{6} \cdot 2\frac{1}{5} =$ _____

10. $4\frac{1}{4} \cdot \frac{3}{8} =$ _____

Circle all the names that describe the shape.

11.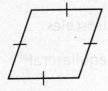

12.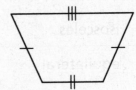

quadrilateral	trapezoid		quadrilateral	trapezoid
parallelogram	rhombus		parallelogram	rhombus
rectangle	square		rectangle	square

13. **Stretch Your Thinking** The sum of the lengths of any two sides of a triangle must be greater than the length of the third side. List three side lengths that will form a triangle. Use a ruler and draw the triangle.

_____

Attributes of Triangles

Homework

Draw a shape that fits the description. Mark all congruent segments and right angles.

1. an open shape made up of one or more curves

2. a concave quadrilateral with an acute angle and exactly two congruent sides

3. a closed shape that is not a polygon made entirely of segments

4. a convex pentagon with two parallel sides and two perpendicular sides

5. a concave hexagon with two pairs of congruent sides

6. a quadrilateral with four congruent sides that is not regular

Remembering

Simplify. Follow the Order of Operations.

1. $61 - 300 \div 6$

2. $0.8 \div (0.09 - 0.07)$

3. $4 \cdot 9 - 12 \div 3$

4. $(\frac{5}{12} + \frac{3}{4}) \cdot 12$

5. $44 + 29 - 13 + 34$

6. $100 \div (6 - 2) \cdot 5$

Circle all the names that describe the shape.

7.

acute   scalene

right   isosceles

obtuse   equilateral

8.

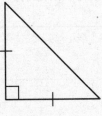

acute   scalene

right   isosceles

obtuse   equilateral

9. Stretch Your Thinking Write a description of
a two-dimensional shape and then draw
the shape.

_____

Name _____   **Date** _____

Homework

Solve.

1. On the grid below, draw and label an aquarium
   shaped like a rectangular prism with a volume of
   8,000 cubic inches. (Hint: A cube is a rectangular
   prism, and $2 \times 2 \times 2 = 8$.)

2. Calculate the perimeter of the top of your
   aquarium. Then calculate the area of its base.

   $P =$ _____

   $A =$ _____

3. The rectangular prism you drew for Problem 1
   is not the only rectangular prism that has a
   volume of 8,000 cubic inches. Other prisms are
   possible. On the grid below, use a new color
   and draw a different rectangular prism that
   has a volume of 8,000 cubic inches.

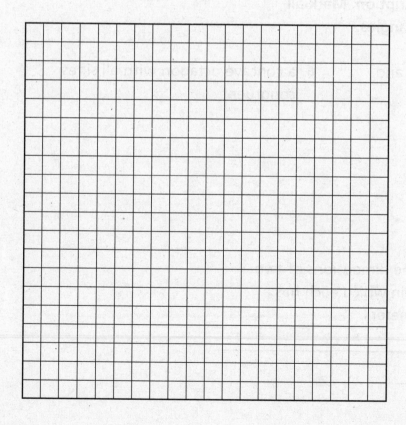

© Houghton Mifflin Harcourt Publishing Company

Remembering

Complete the pattern.

1. $22 \times 10^1 = 22 \times 10 =$ _____

   $22 \times 10^2 = 22 \times 100 =$ _____

   $22 \times 10^3 = 22 \times 1,000 =$ _____

   $22 \times 10^4 = 22 \times 10,000 =$ _____

2. $412 \times 10^1 =$ _____ $= 4,120$

   $412 \times 10^2 = 412 \times 100 =$ _____

   $412 \times 10^3 =$ _____ $= 412,000$

   $412 \times 10^4 = 412 \times 10,000 =$ _____

3. $56 \times 10^1 =$ _____ $= 560$

   $56 \times 10^2 =$ _____ $= 5,600$

   $56 \times 10^3 =$ _____ $= 56,000$

   $56 \times 10^4 =$ _____ $= 560,000$

4. $8 \times 10^1 = 8 \times 10 =$ _____

   $8 \times 10^2 = 8 \times 100 =$ _____

   $8 \times 10^3 = 8 \times 1,000 =$ _____

   $8 \times 10^4 = 8 \times 10,000 =$ _____

Draw a shape that fits the description. Mark all congruent segments and right angles.

5. a triangle with a right angle and exactly two congruent sides

6. a concave octagon with all sides congruent

7. **Stretch Your Thinking** List the dimensions of two different rectangular prisms in which each has a volume of 6,600 cubic centimeters.

   _____

   _____

Focus on Mathematical Practices